This Conversation

This Conversation

Christopher Bogart

A Publication of The Poetry Box®

Poems ©2022 Christopher Bogart
All rights reserved.

Editing & Book Design by Shawn Aveningo Sanders
Cover Design & Photography by Robert R. Sanders

No part of this book may be reproduced in any manner whatsoever without permission from the author, except in the case of brief quotations embodied in critical essays, reviews and articles.

ISBN: 978-1-956285-12-3
Library of Congress Control Number: 2022903914
Printed in the United States of America.
Wholesale Distribution via Ingram.

Published by The Poetry Box®, June 2022
Portland, Oregon
ThePoetryBox.com

Dedicated to:

Emmett Till, George Stinney, Eric Garner, John Crawford III, Michael Brown, Ezell Ford, Dante Parker, Michelle Cusseaux, Laquan McDonald, Tanisha Anderson, Akai Gurley, Tamir Rice, Rumain Brisbon, Jermane Reid, George Mann, Matthew Ajibade, Frank Smart, Natasha McKenna, Tony Robinson, Anthony Hill, Mya Hall, Phillip White, Eric Harris, Walter Scott, William Chapman II, Aexia Christian, Brendon Glenn, Victor Manue LaRosa, Jonathan Sanders, Freddie Blue, Joseph Mann, Salvado Ellswood, Sandra Bland, Albert Joseph Davis, Darrius Stewart, Billy Ray Davis, Samuel Dubois, Michael Sabbie, Brian Keith Day, Christian Taylor, Troy Robinson, Asshams Pharaoh Manley, Felix Kumi, Keith Harrison McLeod, Junior Prosper, Lamontez Jones, Paterson Brown, Dominic Hutchinson, Anthony Ashford, Alonzo Smith, Tyree Crawford, India Kager, La'Vante Biggs, Michael Lee Marshall, Jamar Clark, Richard Perkins, Nathaniel Harris Pickett, Benni Lee Tignor, Miguel Espinal, Michael Noel, Kevin Matthews, Bettie Jones, Quintonio Legrier, Keith Childress Jr., Janet Wilson, Randy Nelson, Antroinie Scott, Wendell Celestine, David Joseph, Caan Roquemore, Dyzhawn Perkins, Christopher Davis, Marco Loud, Peter Gaines, Torrey Robinson, Darius Robinson, Kevin Hicks, Mary Truxillo, Demarcus Semer, Wilie Tillman, Terril Thomas, Sylvie Smith, Alton Sterling, Philandro Castile, Terence Crutcher, Paul O'Neal, Ateria Woods, Jordan Edwards, Aaron Bailey, Ronell Foster, Stephon Clark, Antwon Rose II, Botham Jean, Pamela Turner, Dominique Clayton, Atatiana Jefferson, Christopher Whitfield, Christopher McCorvey, Eric Reason, Kionte Spencer, Michael Lorenzo Dean, Trayvon Martin, Freddie Gray, Ahmaud Arbery, Tony McDade, Brionna Taylor, George Floyd, Elijah McClain, Nicholas Heyward, Casey Goodson Jr, Andre Hill, Daunte Wright

...and all those unnamed young men and women of color who were somebody's children and who died solely because of the color of their skin.

No man can put a chain about the ankle of his fellow man without at last finding the other end fastened about his own neck.

—Frederick Douglass, Speech at Civil Rights Mass Meeting, Washington, DC, October 22, 1883

If you can convince the lowest white man he's better than the best colored man, he won't notice you're picking his pocket. Hell, give him somebody to look down on, and he'll empty his pockets for you.

—Lyndon B. Johnson, 1963

I might be poor white trash, but at least I ain't no ▬!

—Poor Southern white sharecropper, 1965

It's amazing why we keep loving this country, and this country does not love us back.

—Doc Rivers, Coach of The Los Angeles Clippers, August 26, 2020

Contents

Letter to the Reader	11
Introduction	13
Preface	15
This Conversation: When?	17
A Civil Discourse: First Skirmish	19
Carefully Taught	22
A Civil Discourse: Second Skirmish	24
Ọna Arin (Middle Passage)	27
A Civil Discourse: Third Skirmish	30
One Drop	33
A Civil Discourse: Fourth Skirmish	35
Privilege	38
A Civil Discourse: Fifth Skirmish	39
A Sonnet in Honor of Emmett Till	41
A Civil Discourse: Sixth Skirmish	43
Taught to Be Careful	48
A Civil Discourse: Seventh Skirmish	51
Skin in the Game	54
A Civil Discourse: Eighth Skirmish	55
This Conversation: Who?	58
Notes	63
Acknowledgments	65
Early Praise for *This Conversation*	69
About the Author	71

Letter to the Reader

I wrote this book of poetry, my fellow white Americans and anyone else who chooses to read it, to begin a dialogue with you about race, to share my own experiences, to inform, hopefully to enlighten, and ultimately to convince those of you with whom I share a skin color, and any and all others who might need to hear what these poems are saying, that we must accept that the America of the future has to be different from the America of the past, different even from the America of the present.

This Conversation that I am beginning with you today must ultimately change the America in which we live by making our country finally live up to the promises that our Founding Fathers had made in the Declaration of Independence, the Constitution of the United States, the Fourteenth and the Fifteenth Amendments, the Civil Rights Act of 1964, and the Voting Rights Act of 1965. All these laws, and their protections and rights, are already codified into the body of laws that governs our nation. However, they are not yet enshrined in our hearts. It is your minds, my fellow white Americans, and, more importantly, your hearts, that I will be talking to today in this book of poetry.

While I use the paradigm of an accidental meeting between two strangers at a local bar, it is through this device that I will be speaking to all of you to encourage you to think about the problem of systemic racism, and to encourage you to have this conversation with others.

It is true that we cannot change the past, but we must change the present. We must remove all barriers in our laws, in our behavior and, most importantly, in our hearts. Only then will we be able to live up to the words inscribed in the Declaration of Independence two-hundred and forty-four years ago: "We hold these truths to be self-evident, that all men are created equal, that they are endowed by their Creator with certain unalienable Rights, that among these are Life, Liberty and the pursuit of Happiness."

This Conversation we will have today must be the beginning of the last conversation we will ever need to have about race. Forty-one-millions of our fellow citizens, our Black brothers and sisters, are depending on us.

—Christopher Bogart

Introduction

This *Conversation*, the one we are starting today, is not the first conversation that we, as Americans, have had on the topic of racism—not by a longshot. In his speech in Philadelphia on March 18, 2008, in reference to The Declaration of Independence, President Barack Obama stated:

It was stained by this nation's original sin of slavery, a question that divided the colonies and brought the convention to a stalemate until the founders chose to allow the slave trade to continue for at least twenty more years, and to leave any final resolution to future generations.

While conversations on this topic were being held in abolition meetings in the North, and in churches all over the colonies, the future of slavery, the institutionalization of America's original sin that had begun these conversations, eventually led to a civil war to decide the issue once and for all. It cost the country over 750,000 human lives. And still, only part of the problem was solved. It would take another hundred years of denial before the conversation about race would be raised again—but this time by the people of color who were its victims.

In those hundred years after the ink had dried on The Emancipation Proclamation of 1863 (and on the 13th Amendment to the Constitution of the United States in 1865), institutions built to support a segregation of the races hardened like a stone wall around African Americans, denying them most of the freedoms that should have been afforded to them by full citizenship and participation in a fully integrated society. It would take Dr. Martin Luther King, Jr. and the leaders of the Civil Rights Movement to finally force the U.S. Congress to spell out and codify these rights in the Civil Rights Act of 1964 and the Voting Rights Act of 1965, and to begin the integration of schools and universities throughout the North as well as the South. Yet even this legislation was not enough. These laws might have been put into place to protect the legal rights of African Americans, but the hearts and minds of many white Americans were still hardened against their full equality.

Today there are some of us who now see reasons for cautious optimism in the evidence of what seems to be a changing paradigm in

[. . .]

American society. As recently as thirty years ago, the murder of a young Black man at the hands of the law would have produced an isolated and exclusively Black response. However, the murder of George Perry Floyd at the hands of the Minneapolis Police on May 25, 2020, produced a wave of demonstrations in every major city and town throughout America—and, indeed, throughout a majority of the countries of the world. And in all of these demonstrations, under the banner of "Black Lives Matter," an equal number of White, Asian, Latinx and Native Americans marched arm in arm and in solidarity with their African American brothers and sisters. This is no longer just an African American problem—but an American problem.

It is these events, as well as the promises of full equality long overdue for the African American community, that demand that this conversation be had now.

Preface

This book is divided into two forms of poetry: poetic dialogue written in free verse, and a variety of traditional as well as non-traditional forms of poetry (see Notes). According to the *Oxford Dictionary of the English Language*, the adjective *civil* can mean two different things. In reference to our Civil War, the dictionary defines *civil* as "relating to ordinary citizens and their concerns." As it relates to behavior, it is defined as "courteous and polite."

I am using the first definition when I use it to refer to the political split in our society today. However, when I couple it with the word "discourse," I am referring to its second definition as well. I refer to each discourse, not as a battle, but as a skirmish, a civil conversation of differing opinions to enlighten and resolve the two very different polarities that, as they were almost 160 years ago, are now tearing our country apart.

Our 35th president, John Fitzgerald Kennedy, once asked "If not us, who? If not now, when?" I begin this collection of poems with his second question to indicate in no uncertain terms that this conversation must be had now. And I end this collection with the first question to state we are each responsible for having this conversation so that the systemic racism that has plagued our country since the arrival of the first African captive in 1619, finally comes to an end.

In his book, *Uncomfortable Conversations with a Black Man*, Emanuel Acho, former linebacker for the Philadelphia Eagles, encourages white people to speak to each other, to have this very important conversation about the treatment of his Black brothers and sisters. "It's going to take courageous, informed, empathetic, committed white people to challenge their racial peers who rely on white talk. If your goal is to fight racism, to help foster an America that isn't built on white privilege, then you'll have to do your part."

I have written this book of poems to have this conversation as Emanuel Acho suggests. "To do my part." And to begin *This Conversation* now.

This Conversation: When?

If not now, when?
　　　　—President John Fitzgerald Kennedy (1962)

this conversation we're starting today
must not end at the end of this day—
　　　　not end with the last
　　　　hand lettered sign
writ in some Black brother's blood,
not end with the last car burning in anguish,
not end with the last mile marched in frustration,
nor end with the last tear shed in stark sorrow
over another young Black brother's grave.

this conversation we're starting today
must be the start of a brand-new beginning—
　　　　not like the beginning
　　　　of past conversations
　　　　abandoned long before they'd begun.

not the conversation that was set to be settled
　　　　by abolition,
　　　　by emancipation,
　　　　by civil war.

nor even the last conversation
of commitment abandoned
to lies long before it was borne
　　　　in the marching,
　　　　in the jailing,
　　　　in the shooting,
　　　　and the dying
　　　　over sixty years ago.

[. . .]

this conversation
we're starting today
        must begin with one question
        that has echoed eternal
        in every Black church
        and from every Black voice
        from the north to the south,
        from the east and the west,
        and from each generation
        to the next and the next:
for that one eternal question:
        how long?
can no longer be answered:
        not long.

no. this conversation we will start here today
must finally answer
this one simple question
at last and forever,
and for all time eternal
        with only one answer—
        and that answer
        needs to be

        Now.

A Civil Discourse: First Skirmish

It was just an ordinary night at the bar that sat at the edge of our town.
The white noise of conversation was punctuated by the clinking of glasses and
The dull thud of bottled beers being dropped onto cardboard mats.

Suddenly, I felt a tap on my shoulder.
Excuse me, a voice said as he pulled out the stool,
Is anyone sitting here?

There is now, I replied.

He sat down by my side, and signaled the bartender for a beer.
I went back to watching the overhead screen and the demonstrators
Marching to seek justice for the death of George Floyd.

The bartender came over, asked, "What'll you have?"
The man on the stool, eyes glued to the screen, pointed to my bottle of beer.
Within a fast minute, the bartender returned, placed the cold beer on a mat.

The man on the stool raised his beer to his lips, took a sip,
Then spoke to the screen without turning to me.
*What d'ya think about what's going on
In the streets of America these days?*

What do you think? I asked him.

He sat for a moment in silent reflection,
His cold beer clasped firm in his hand.

Why are you answering my question with a question?
He took a long hit of his beer.

Do you really need to know what I think? I asked him.
Don't you know what the answer should be?

*Easy Buddy!
Just trying to make conversation.*

[. . .]

He paused—
Then took another hit.

Ok, he stated, when I failed to reply,
I don't get their beef.
And I don't know what that beef
Has to do with me.

Couldn't say, I respond,
I'm just drinking my beer.

But…

Maybe your use of *"they"* is the dead give-away.
Don't you think that that word might be the problem here?

Well, aren't they "they" as opposed to us?
He pointed the neck of his beer toward the screen.

Well, I replied. I thought we were both on the same side.
I thought that "us" was really just "we."

You know what I mean,
He replied in frustration,
I mean that you and I are both the same race
So it's really just us that's "we."

I know what you mean.
I took a sip of my beer.
But look at that screen.
There's Black and there's white,
Marching together in the same common cause.
Don't you think that they think
Of themselves as "we?"

But they're not all "white,"
He quickly insisted,
Not like you and like me.

And how does that matter?
I asked in reply.

They both have two arms, two legs,
Have a mother and father,
And a heart that beats
With the same red blood
As we.

Yeah. I know, but...

Or are you saying they're not human?
Is that what you believe?

No, he answered quickly.
Then he paused for a moment,
*I guess I just look at "them"
As different from me.*

Why, I asked?

I guess that's just the way I was taught.

I get that,
I replied.
And, in a way, so was I.

But maybe we're overdue to learn something new,
Something just a little less judgmentally fraught—
Something different,
From what we once thought was so true—
From what we were once
So very carefully taught.

Carefully Taught

You've got to be taught before it's too late
Before you are six, or seven, or eight
To hate all the people your relatives hate
　　　—from "Carefully Taught," *South Pacific*,
　Richard Rodgers and Oscar Hammerstein (1949)

Eeny, Meeny, Miny, Moe.
Catch a ▮▮▮ by the toe.
If he hollers, let him go.
Eeny, Meeny, Miny Moe.

When Dad took me to Ebbets Field
To see the Dodgers play,
We had to sit in ▮▮▮ Heaven
Because we couldn't pay.

My cousin contended
That behavior was the trigger:
"If he acts like a ▮▮▮,
I'll call him a ▮▮▮!

Mom hated Martin Luther King.
She called him Martin Luther ▮▮▮.
She wouldn't use that awful word,
When guests were in our living room.

Have your Black college friend come here to visit?
Absolutely no way!
Having a ▮▮▮ in our neighborhood?
What would the neighbors say?

We're not born with these biases.
They're not a part of our DNA.
We learn them from those whom we most trust—

We learn them from those we were taught to obey.

But when we reach maturity,
It's our responsibility
To rethink all that we once thought—
What we were once so carefully taught.

A Civil Discourse: Second Skirmish

You know, I was taught I was better than "them"
He said as he shifted his stool.

And why do you think you were taught that, I asked him?

I don't know, he replied.
Maybe 'cause they came
From the world's other side,
You know, where they wore loin cloths,
Hunted food in the jungles,
Carried long sharp spears.

And that's your understanding of African culture:
Loin cloths, food hunting, and spears?

So what are you trying to tell me then, now?
That it was more like Wakanda?
With cities, and science labs,
And African cultural museums?

You know, of course, Wakanda doesn't exist.

A self-satisfied smirk spread over his face.

But maybe you should know
What we once called the Dark Continent
Was really bright with civilizations,
With empires and cultures
That dated way back
Over four thousand years.

As a matter of fact,
That very continent
We thought was so dark,
Was actually home to universities
That came into existence

Before the first one in Europe
By over one hundred years.

Does that sound to you that their native land
Was once only jungles, and loincloths, and spears?

Well, I guess we thought that
Because once they had gotten here,
We saw them only as slaves.
He mused to himself.
We saw them only as property.

And whose fault do you think that was?
I asked him.

Well, I know one thing for sure,
His voice tensed
As he shot back, defensively,
It sure as hell wasn't mine!

I never owned slaves.
Nor my ancestors, neither.
My dad's family came from Ireland,
My mother's, from Greece.
They landed here broke.
Slaved from sunrise to sunset
On construction sites and in factories.
Barely making ends meet.

No, you're right, I said, much to his surprise,
You and I weren't there then,
And neither were "they."

We weren't there
When their ancestors were first brought here.
We weren't there
When their families were robbed, beaten and sold.
So why should we feel guilty, right?
We're not responsible!

[. . .]

Right, he agreed, so sure of himself.

No, we shouldn't feel guilty—
At least that's what we've been told.

You just said it, he reminded me.
You just said that we weren't there.

Okay, I replied, but even if we weren't,
Should we care any less?

For all of the years
Since their families were freed—
They've lived lives that were stunted.
As our families thrived,
Theirs barely survived.

They weren't allowed to live in neighborhoods we lived in.
They were confined to a second-class world of their own,
Denied jobs. Denied housing, education. Denied justice
In an America that they desperately wanted to call home.

Shouldn't we take at least some responsibility
For what our ancestors had first begun,
For what these people have suffered
All these years since those days:
Since those were the lives
That we forced "them" to live,
For generation after generation
As victims of what was really
Our original sin?

Ọna Arin (Middle Passage)

I've known rivers:
I've known rivers ancient as the world and older than the flow
Of human blood in human veins.
My soul has grown deep like the rivers.

—Langston Hughes, "The Negro Speaks of Rivers"

Just bury me in the ocean,
with my ancestors that jumped from the ships . . .
'cause they knew death was better than bondage.

—Killmonger, *Black Panther* (Ryan Coogler, Joe Robert Cole)

I. *Ilu abinbi/Ominira*
(Homeland/Freedom)

Spiked spears reached up to strike the skies of Manden Kuruowca.
Its capital of Timbuktu stretched out to both horizons.
The kingdom of the richest man the world has ever known–
The Empire of Mali—once the great gold world of
Mansa Musa—grandest emperor in all of Africa.
Thousands of *griots* once sang songs and told tales to spread the word
Of brave Mandinka warriors, their language and their laws.

Brave Mandinka warriors spread language and spread laws.
Each warrior, by law, had to be *horon,* of freemen cast.
And with the help of river clans, they kept the Mali peace.
Their Sankara Madrassa held a million manuscripts,
The largest library in the world since Alexandria.
The shadows of spiked spears around the Great Djenne Mosque
Stretched out from Mali's desert sands to Mali's Ocean Sea.

[. . .]

II. Òkun/Kikú
(Ocean/Death)

The coast of Mali's Ocean Sea was dotted with its ports.
The slave ships docked, their sails still furled, awaited human cargo.
Of twenty-million captured from the land's interior,
Half don't survive the tortuous journey to the western coast.
Once they arrived at Mali's ports, their "wooly" heads were shaved,
Their naked backs were seared with brands that glowed in dark ships' holds,
Their hands and feet were clapped in irons before the ships depart.

Their limbs were shackled, hand and foot, five hundred in each hold,
The air, a fetid bouillabaisse of human sweat and human waste.
Many just refused to eat. The speculum performed its task.
Some died slowly of bloody flux. Some jumped into the waves.
Two million skulls—two million souls—lie on Atlantic's ocean floor.
A dead body cannot receive a double punishment.
If there's not cloth to cover it, they'll always be the sea.

III. *Ominira padanu/Awọn iran ti sọnu*
(Freedom lost/Generations lost)

Generations of Africans were placed upon the block.
Once proud *horon*, now property, were bought and sold in lots.
They worked from dawn till after dusk for six days of each week.
They lived in one room cabins, slept on straw, little to eat.
Some were given shoes to wear. Most walked on their bare feet.
White overseers controlled their days. Sleep was their sole release.
For every day of every year, this life would be their destiny.

As generations came and went—their lives remained the same,
Forced to live like animals, with first but no last names.
For property did not need names. Their value was their cost.
Families were bought and sold, with no account for human loss.
Forbidden to learn to read or write, an X replaced identity.
Time erased their culture, servitude—their dignity.
And soon, the pride of brave *horon* was struck from human memory.

---

griots: African troubadors.

horon: Freemen

speculum orum: Hinged forceps used to spread the mouth and glottis open to force-feed a slave.

bloody flux: Dysentery

A Civil Discourse: Third Skirmish

Why should I repent? That sin isn't mine.

Maybe not, but neither was English Rule
Or, for that matter,
The potato famine,
Theirs.

What's that supposed to mean?
His question cut through the air.

It was only the Africans
Who were removed from their homelands,
Carried 'cross the Atlantic,
And sold in the Americas—
An ocean away.

It was only the Africans
Who were deemed not-quite human property
In a country called America,
"The land of the free."

And when their four-hundred-year diaspora was over,
They were stuck in a land where they were no longer wanted,
In a land that had separated them
Hundreds of years ago
From their culture,
And their ancestry.

See,
The real difference is
That your ancestors chose
To cross the Atlantic,
And when they arrived,
Their first sight of our land was
The Statue of Liberty,
A land full of opportunities,

A land free from harm.

The first sight of our land that these Africans saw
Were the worn wooden platforms
Of slave sellers' stalls
That were crudely erected
At the water's edge.
No opportunities awaited them there,
Only servitude,
And heartache,
And chains.

*America didn't always greet us
With open arms either.
There were once signs that said
"No dogs and Irishmen here!"*

You're right, I replied,
In the late 1800s,
But, sooner than later,
Those signs disappeared.

Yet those same racist signs,
A hundred years later,
Were still up and hanging
For all folks of color
All over the South
On fountains,
On bathrooms,
And in the windows of stores
In an effort by whites
To keep the Blacks out.

And do you know why those signs remained? I asked him.

No, he replied, *but I have a feeling you'll tell me.*

It's really quite simple.
It's because our faces were white,

[. . .]

While theirs were black and brown.
Ours were pure white,
As snow on the mountains,
And white is always white,
Its supremacy rarely doubted.

But though black comes in all shades,
From jet black to light brown,
Black's always black.
There's no middle ground.

One Drop

I got dark, I got evil that rot
Inside my DNA.
I got loyalty, I got royalty
Inside my DNA

    —Kendrick Lamar, "DNA," *Damn*

One
Black drop
Is all it takes
To put the ▮▮▮▮▮
In his place,
To make a white skin
Crackle black,
To label him,
To push him back
Into the dark
And bottomless hold
Where Black is Black—
And Sold is Sold.

If Black blood's all that powerful,
Why ain't it that supreme?

One
Black drop
Just one Black drop from
One Black vein
Will change
The face
Of what we claim—
The Master Race—
Supremacy,
What sense of science
Makes DNA when

[. . .]

Just one drop
Washes all away
Into the wooden galley's hold
To make them stay—
To pay the price
They've always paid.

If Black blood's all that powerful,
Why ain't it that supreme?

So what then makes
Supremacy
And who decides
What it's to be?
The royalty?
The loyalty?
Or the inky dark
Of one Black drop
Just one Black drop
Of ▮▮▮▮ DNA?

Why,
If Black blood's all that powerful,
Ain't it also that supreme?

A Civil Discourse: Fourth Skirmish

How is that my fault?
And what could I do about that?

Have we not profited
From their Black disadvantage?
Isn't that our advantage,
Our lily-white skin?

Oh, so now you're going to claim it's all about privilege?

Are you really going to claim that with white you don't win?

I work very hard for what I achieve.

I believe you, I replied, but then so have they.
Only for you and I, the sky is the limit,
But for them, they're still thwarted,
Held back "in their place."

Many of us had to overcome setbacks.
It's all a part of our human fate.

Yeah, but none of those setbacks
That you had to face
Had to do with your color,
Had to do with your race.

He turned from me in mute frustration,
Raised his bottle of beer, took a healthy swig.

Listen!
All I'm trying to say is that
These descendants of enslaved people
Have witnessed wave after wave
Of white immigration,
Generation after generation,

[. . .]

Watching whites raise their families,
Sending their kids off to college,
Giving them chance after chance
To achieve their own dreams.

Yet the very same people
Who built this America,
Whose blood's in our fields,
In our buildings' foundations,
Have yet to achieve
Their American Dream.

Hell, we've made racism a monument
In this country of monuments,
A ritual,
A sacrament,
One we've benefited from now
For over four hundred years.

But their fingerprints are on our bread,
Their footprints, on our grapes.
When do we finally
Take responsibility,
To ask the vintner
How the wine has been made?

Ok, he smiled as he turned back to me.
Even though what you're saying
Sounds just a bit like poetry,
I understand the point you're making
About white supremacy.
But how is it a "privilege" to be white—
Isn't white privilege just a fallacy?

You're almost right!

It's not an accurate phrase,
But not for the reason you might think.
To be treated with respect as human beings

Should not be looked upon as privilege
But as a right,
A right that's extended
To the whole human race.

To be treated as less,
Because of race,
And to be treated that way
For over four hundred years,
Is really Black disadvantage and
Is truly our national disgrace!

I lifted my hand up.
I pointed at the screen.

They're just looking to be treated
The same way as we.
It's this disadvantage that we have to change!
They need to be treated with full equality!

Don't you see?
They're tired
Of being treated
As "other."
They just want to
Be treated
As "we."

Privilege

Whiteness—even as a construction and mirage—has informed their notion of America and identity and offered them privilege, the primary one being the privilege of being inherently normal, standard, and legal.

—Ibram X. Kendi, *How to Be an Antiracist*

We're not asking you to shoot them like you shoot us.
We're asking you NOT to shoot us like you DON'T shoot them!

—Leslie Jones/Comedian (Twitter, January 7, 2021)

    Is privilege about advantage to one, or disadvantage to others?
    If two workers are given an equal wage for an equal day's work,

        But one is given a bonus as well as his wage,
        Would that bonus be unfair? Or just be "more?"

    If there were no bonus—would there be a "more?"
    And if there were no "more," would there be advantage?

        But what if one worker were paid a just wage, and the other,
        Paid a lot less for the same job? Would that be fair?

    Is it more about the "more?"
    Or is it really more about the "less?"

        Our rights are wages. Shouldn't they be equal and fair?
        Equal and fair for all of our citizens, regardless of race.

    For the lack of equality is not really about advantage for some,
    But about disadvantage for others.

A Civil Discourse: Fifth Skirmish

Once I had made my point, we sat there in silence,
Both of us staring at the flickering screen.

Then my new beer buddy broke that silence.
He seemed now to have thought of a new issue, it seemed:

Black Lives Matter, he stated simply.
What's that supposed to mean?

I'd have thought that that would be obvious, I stated.
What do you think it means?

See, I don't understand why only Black lives should matter.
How about blue lives? Don't they matter too?
I just thought that all lives would matter.
That's all that I'm saying.
Just like Black lives do.

I paused briefly to digest his latest white grievance,
And to gather my thoughts for a moment or two.

Ok, I said.
What if I told you
I had terminal cancer,
And that I had only
Six months to live?

He turned to me quickly.

I'm so sorry buddy.
I never would have thought…

I interrupted his speech before he could finish.

Why should you be upset?
Lots of people have cancer.

[. . .]

Why should the life
Of one stranger you just met
Matter so much to you?

What's one life?
Don't all lives matter?

Besides, sitting here,
What could you do?

He just sat there for a moment
Stewing in silence,
Then said, *But what about blue lives?*
Don't blue lives matter too?

Sure, Blue lives matter.
It's a dangerous occupation
But police officers choose to put on the blue.
They're paid to put their life on the line
To make a living,
That's what they chose to do.

But those Black folks on that screen,
Now that's an entirely different matter.
They don't choose to be Black.
And, against armed police,
They can't fight back.
It seems it's more of a hazard
To have Black skin
And to live in America
Than to choose to be dressed in Blue.

My new buddy just stared at the screen
At the Black and white protesters,
Marching in silence,
Mourning the death
Of yet another Black man.

A Sonnet in Honor of Emmett Till

> *Emmett Till*
> *Won't be still.*
> —James Emanuel, "Emmett Till," (1963)

Nicholas Heyward was shot and killed while playing cops and robbers.
"We're only playing," were his last words. Cops just couldn't be bothered.

Kiwane Carrington held down when a cop's gun accidentally went off.
Even though Kiwane had done no wrong, another Black life was lost.

Aiyana Jones was in her bed when shot and died instantly.
The cops barged in, their guns ablaze. It was being filmed for TV.

Treyvon Martin, armed with Skittles and an Arizona Iced Tea
Gunned down by a "neighborhood volunteer," and then set free.

Cameron Tillman, played in a house with the owner's permission.
It took Cameron 15 minutes to die. He was offered no assistance.

Tamir Rice was shot by a cop while playing in a Cleveland park.
Tamir had a toy. The cop didn't care. He fired before the car even stopped.

Tyre King was five feet tall and weighed less than one hundred pounds.
Police mistook him for a robber, peppered his body with rounds.

Jordan Edwards was leaving a party when he was savagely gunned down.
He sat in his car. He was shot in the head. No believable reason was found.

Stephon Clark was shot in the dark, six times in his back alone.
Police said he was holding a gun. All they found was his phone.

Botham Jean was surprised in his flat by an off-duty cop on the scene.
She shot. Said it was "self-defense." But the flat wasn't hers. It was Jean's.

Deaunta Farrow raised his hands but the cops shot off half a clip.
They said they thought they saw a gun. He had a bag of chips.

[. . .]

Elijah McClain was walking home when a cop snuffed out his life with a knee. "I'm just different. That's all," he pleaded. His last words were "Forgive me."

Ahmaud Arbery, was jogging in a white suburb as two men drive up in a car. They shot him three times in the hand and chest. He didn't jog very far.

Casey Goodson was shot in the back entering his grandmother's home. All he carried was a Subway sandwich. No gun. No Skittles. No phone.

                        ~

In the summer of 1955, they lynched 14-year-old Emmet Till,
And even though it was many years ago, his memory just won't be still.

Ages of the Victims: Nicholas Heyward (13), Kiwane Carrington (15), Aiyana Jones (7), Treyvon Martin (17), Cameron Tillman (14), Tamir Rice (12), Tyre King (13,) Jordan Edwards (15), Stephon Clark (22), Botham Jean (26), Deaunta Farrow (13), Elijah McClain (23), Ahmaud Arbery (25), and Casey Goodson (23).

A Civil Discourse: Sixth Skirmish

He sat there quietly for a minute,
Gazing at the TV screen
With the sound turned way down,
Then broke his stare,
Raised his hand in the air and waved,
Bartender, give my friend and me another round.

The bartender returned with the necks of two beers
Gripped firmly between the fingers of his right hand.
He placed the beers down.
My friend gripped his fingers round
One cold beer, slid the other 'cross to me.

You seem pretty passionate 'bout this topic, buddy.
You got some skin in this game?

Don't you have people of color in your life?
Black friends, Black coworkers?
Maybe just a few?

I work with a few guys.
Maybe they're friends.
Or acquaintances.
Sometimes we eat on the same shift.
He wrapped his two fingers around the beer bottle's neck,
Tipped the opening up to his lips.

Have you ever asked any of them to your home,
Socialized with their families,
Or their families with yours?

Why you asking me these questions?
He said, somewhat annoyed.
I really don't get the point.

[. . .]

So I've never invited them to dinner.
What is it you're trying to prove?
He turned his back to the screen,
Turned around to face me.
What's it to you?

It's simple.
I'm trying to show you
You're choosing to live
In a white-only world.
Your only association
With people of color
Isn't social.
It's accidental.
You and those coworkers
Live in two different worlds.

It's no wonder you say
That you don't understand "them."
You don't even know "them."
And you've never given
"Them" the chance
To know you.

Why is it so important who I know and who I don't know?
Two hours ago, I didn't even know you!

You're making my point for me, my friend.
I raised my bottle in a kind of a toast,
Then took a sip of my beer.

Let me ask you another question:
When you came into the bar two hours ago,
If the only stool not taken
Was next to a Black man,
Would you have taken the stool anyway?
Treated him to a beer?

I don't know what I would have done.

*But it just didn't happen
So why make an issue of it?
Why not just sit back
And drink our beers?*

Don't you see?
How can you be so very sure
Of what you believe
If what you believe is based
On what you see on TV?

*I'm not sure I understand what you're saying,
And what you expect me to do?*

Do you have any children?

Yeah. Sure. I have two boys.

How old are they?

*One's seventeen.
The other's twenty-two.*

Do they have any friends
Who are not white?

Well, he sat and thought for a minute
*To tell you the truth,
I really don't know.
The younger one's on his high school football team.
The older one's in the Army,
So I guess so.*

He sat and thought a little while.
While he scraped at the label of his beer with his nail.

*I guess my young son probably does
Since he's on the school football team.
Many of his fellow players*

[. . .]

Are probably Black.

As for my oldest son…

He sank deep into thought,
His nail digging deeper
Into the wet label of his beer.

Yeah. I guess I see your point.
My boys must have at least a few Black friends,
Friends that really don't look like them.

Have they ever brought home
Their teammates of color
To introduced to you and to your wife?

No.
Not that I remember.

Why?
Is it because
They don't look like you?

He didn't respond.

Did your boys know
If their Black friends would have been welcome?
Would they have been treated
As guests?

He sat again in silence.
I could almost hear him think.
Suddenly, he stopped peeling,
Put the neck to his lips,
And took another sip.

You know, Black parents have the same worries
About their children
That you and your wife have

About yours:
Are they hanging around
With the right crowd?
Are they careful?
Are they safe?

But the difference is
When your sons go out at night
To a party or on a date,
Your only concern about
Their being stopped by the cops
Is for their safe driving,
Not for their race.

While Black parents have to worry that
Their sons could be stopped
Simply because of
The color of
Their face.

Taught to be Careful

"I got stopped again, Dad. Again! And the cop asked me, 'Who is your P.O.?' And I said, 'What's a P.O.?' and the cop yelled, 'Parole officer!' I was in a suit, Dad! A suit!" A single tear fell down his face.

—Langston, "Black Fathers Share Their Fears and Their Hopes for Their Sons in America Today," *Time Magazine* (June 15, 2018)

You will have to work twice as hard to go half as far.

—Jumy Dapo-Ogunsola, "Commentary: How one Black mother is preparing her son for life in today's world," *Global News* (19 June 2020)

1. *Umoga* (Unity)

My son,
I want you to
listen to me carefully
because there are certain things that
you need to know to get
by in this world
today.

2. *Kujichagulia* (Self-Determination)

While you
may always be
a first-class citizen,
you will always be treated as
second-class citizen
however hard
you try.

3. *Ujima* (Responsibility)

Always
carry ID
for proof of who you are,
and always be extra polite
so you get safely home
to your own bed
at night.

4. *Ujamaa* (Cooperative Economics)

Don't wear
clothes that stand out,
hoodies or baggy pants,
a backwards cap or silk durag
or you'll be taken for
a gangster or
a thug.

5. *Nia* (Purpose)

Always
put both hands on
top of your car's dashboard
where the cops can clearly see them,
and always expect to
get patted down
as well.

[. . .]

6. *Kuumba* (Creativity)

You will
always have to
work twice as hard as your
white skinned fellow classmates and friends,
and do that every day,
to go just half
as far.

7. *Imani* (Faith)

Know this—
that no matter
what others think of you,
you must be proud of who you are.
for if you have this faith,
my son, then you'll
go far.

Civil Discourse: Seventh Skirmish

Do you have kids?
My beer buddy asked me.

Yeah. I do, I replied.
Just one.

A daughter? he asked again.

No. I answered.
A son.

And does your son have any Black friends?
He continued
As he slowly
Sipped his beer.

In fact, he does,
I said, sipping my own.
And brown and white friends too.

And I assume you allow him to bring them all home?

I do, I replied.
Why wouldn't I?

He shrugged his shoulders,
I don't know the answer to that.
I don't know what motivates you.

Remember that race should not be an issue.
But racism—
Well, that has to be carefully taught.

So I guess what you're saying
Is that you're more tolerant than me?
No, my friend

[. . .]

It's not tolerance that's needed here.
What this is really about
Is full-blown acceptance,
Regardless of color.
Regardless of race.
This is the "we" I was talking about,
Rather than the "us" and the "they."

In a country that should be
A multi-colored tapestry,
It seems today that America's
Just a piece of white cloth.

Full acceptance is the goal
That's been long overdue.
Tolerance is no longer enough.

Don't you want your sons
To grow up in a world
That's different—
And that's nothing
Like ours?

He again sat in silence
For a minute or two,
Staring at his label-less bottle of beer.

What you're asking is a lot for me to understand,
A lot to bite off and to chew.
This goes against everything
I was raised to believe,
Everything I had once thought to be true.

Well then, maybe it's time,
I said, turning to him,
To try out something brand new.

What do you do to make a living?
He suddenly asked me.

I'm a History teacher at your son's high school.

Oh yeah? he looked at me just a little surprised.
Do you know my son?

No. But I'm sure my son knows yours.

Really? he asked, somewhat curiously.
And what makes you think that is true?

Because they were on the same football team.

Really! he responded, somewhat surprised.
*Well then maybe I've met him,
Maybe my son brought him home
One afternoon after school.*

I doubt it, I replied.

He turned to me, asked
Why?

You told me yourself
That your son's not encouraged
To bring his Black teammates
To your home after school.

That's an honor, it seems,
That's reserved just for whites.

It took him a minute.
He squirmed on his stool,
Then suddenly
He turned to me.

Wait!

Your son's Black?

Skin in the Game

> ... *Everyone you love is*
> *As dark, or at least as black.*
>
> —Jericho Brown, "Dark," *The Tradition* (2020)

If only we could share another's skin
And see life through their eyes for just one day
We'd realize we're so much more than kin.

We'd only need one drop of melanin
To understand what life is like as "they,"
If only we could share another's skin.

One day, one drop for every citizen
In every town across the USA
Would make us realize we're more than kin.

We'd learn, at least, that white's not sovereign
But equal to all colors, on that day,
If only we could share another's skin

They've paid the price in suffering for our sin,
Their generations watched their dreams delayed,
Until we learn we're so much more than kin.

It's time for us to finally welcome in
Our kin of color, cast so far away.
If only we could share another's skin
We'd understand we're so much more than kin.

A Civil Discourse: Eighth Skirmish

Yes, my son is Black,

I don't know what it is I should say.

You don't need to say anything.
You've already said it.

He took a sip of his beer.
He thought for a while.

You know, he said as he turned to me,
*I think I might finally
Get what you're saying!
Your own family isn't "us" or "them."
Your family's really "we,"
So all our families should also
Be "we."*

Then he stopped for a minute
To think about what he had just said.
*And since we're really all family,
Then shouldn't we all really be "we?"*

I looked at him, then smiled,
It seemed to me that pronouns
Was where this conversation had begun.

He smiled in return as
I rose from my stool.

I have to go home now.
I have dinner to make.
I want to spend some time with my son.
He has only a few more weeks to go
Before he starts college this fall.

[. . .]

*You've given me a lot
To think about.*

He paused briefly,
Looked down at his hands,

Then turned to me
Suddenly,
And asked
Why don't you and your son…

I stopped him.

That's really a very generous offer
And a great way for you to begin,
But why not save that thought
For another day—
When you've given yourself time
For it all to sink in.

*But then who can I talk to?
What should I do next?*

Ask the next guy
That sits down when I leave,
And the next guy after that,
And the next,
Until it's no longer an "us"
Or a "them,"
Just a "we"
That goes way beyond
You and me.

I pushed the wooden stool in toward the bar,
Put my hand on his shoulder,
Patted it briefly,
Then headed for the door.

Maybe we'll meet here another night!

My new friend called out
Optimistically.

Maybe,
I responded, suppressing a smile.
As I opened the door to exit the bar,
A middle-aged Black man grabbed it,
Held it open with one hand.

Thanks. I nodded.
No problem, he responded.
Oh,
He turned back around,
Is the bar real crowded?
Think I can find a seat?

Yep,
In fact,
I'm sure of it, I replied.
There's at least one seat inside
That I know is free.

The door swung closed.

I fished for my keys,
Got into my car,
Turned the key in the ignition
And headed on home.

This Conversation: Who?

If not me, who?
  —President John Fitzgerald Kennedy (1962)

this conversation you've heard here today
is the same conversation that must not go away
    when the last demonstrator
    packs his sign up and leaves
    to go home to his family
    till the next black family grieves
    over the next black life lost
    on the streets of our cities
    this conversation must be the cost.

no, this conversation cannot cease to exist
because what caused this conversation is still in our midst,
    in our thoughts,
    in our attitudes,
    in our choice of friends
    and, while hatred still has a home out there,
    this conversation must never end.

no, this conversation must continue
for as long as it takes
for every single person
in the whole human race
    to accept as truth what we all need to believe
    that all men and women are equal,
    regardless of race, color or creed,
    regardless of gender or orientation,
    that all "them" is "us,"
    nd that all "us" is "we."

until we can be comfortable living in each other's skin,
that we are all the same family, that all of us are kin—
    when the day finally comes

that each feels empathy
so deep within him or herself—
then, and only then,
can we put *This Conversation*
back upon the shelf.

but
until that day arrives
there's much more we have to do—
so many conversations to start,
and the one who needs to start them
is

                                              You.

Notes

The figure of 750,000 Civil War dead in the Introduction to this book comes from the recent research of J. David Hacker's paper, "A Census-Based Count of the Civil War Dead" (2012).

I chose the forms of each of the poems in this collection to be appropriate to their messages:

The two poems that begin and end this collection, "When" and "Who" were written to reflect the immediacy of the need to begin *This Conversation*. Based on the famous phrase by President John Fitzgerald Kennedy "If not me who? If not now, when?" These poems are meant to challenge each of the readers of this collection with "the fierce urgency of now" (Dr. Martin Luther King, Jr. 1967) and the necessity of personal participation.

The central idea of the poem, "Carefully Taught," was taken from a song in a Rogers and Hammerstein musical, *South Pacific*, as a lesson about racism. According to Henry Carrington Bolton in his book, *The Counting-Out Rhymes of Children: A Study of Folk-Lore* (1888), in "Eeny, Meeny, Miny, Moe," the object that you "catch by the toe" is not a tiger. And it wasn't sixty-four years later when I was growing up in Queens, NY. I wrote the whole poem in this simple, child's street rhyme form to indicate how early we are taught to "hate all the people our relatives hate." All of the events/reactions cited in the poem are real experiences from the author's life. The quotes, sadly, are accurate as well. The use of pejorative or racially insensitive words have been ▓▓▓ in this manuscript. The reason I used them at all was to accurately reflect the world in which we once lived; and, in far too many cases, the world in which we still live today. The reader should be able to surmise what the words behind the redactions are by context and rhyme.

The poem, "Ọna Arin (Middle Passage)" is a modified form of a Kwansaba, an African American praise poem that uses the number seven as integral to the form. I have modified it to have seven lines (septastich) but with each line having 14 syllables rather than the seven words. The bilingual titles (Yorùbá/English) are meant to symbolize the "passage" those 12.5 million souls made from Africa to the Americas. The two italicized

[. . .]

lines from the second section of the poem are directly quoted from a Yorùbá Nigerian funeral song, "Where Are You Now?"

"One Drop" was inspired by "DNA," a song by Kendrick Lamar from his Pulitzer Prize winning album, *Damn*. The "One Drop Rule" was actually codified into law in many states. The concept of the law was that, if you have one drop of African-American blood, then the law; and, by extension, society, would consider you black. It is also one of the cornerstones of the theory of white supremacy.

The form of the poem, "Privilege," is a duplex of sorts, a poetic form originated by Jericho Brown in his 2020 Pulitzer Prize award-winning book of poetry, *The Tradition*. In this form, he reimagined a 14-line sonnet; but, as he put it, "I decided to call the form a duplex because something about its repetition and its couplets made me feel like it was a house with two addresses." I also chose it for its use of repetition.

I wrote "The Sonnet in Honor of Emmett Till" as a "double sonnet" to reference Marilyn Nelson's *A Wreath For Emmett Till*, a heroic crown of Petrarchan sonnets to honor the death of Emmett Till, a fourteen year old boy who was lynched by a group of white men in 1955 for allegedly whistling at a white woman. The white woman, Carolyn Bryant, recanted her story in 2017, sixty-two years after Till's death. The "double sonnet" is my own invention. It is composed of fourteen couplets rather than fourteen lines. Each of the fourteen couplets tells the story of one young person of color who was killed by police in an unjustified use of force.

The poem "Taught to Be Careful" is an *Eintou*, or "pearl of wisdom," and is a distinctly African American form of poetry with seven lines to represent the seven days/principles of Kwanzaa with the following syllable count: 2,4,6,8,6,4,2. While the word *kwanzaa* is Swahili for "first fruit," the subtitles (named for the seven principals of Kwanzaa) are in the Kiswahili language. "Taught to Be Careful" was inspired by "Commentary: How one Black mother is preparing her son for life in today's world" by Jumy Dapo-Ogunsola in the *Global News* and published on 19 June 2020.

The poem "Skin in the Game" was written as a villanelle and inspired by a number of sources (the primary one being Joe South's "Walk a Mile in My Shoes," 1970), and by John Howard Griffin's book, *Black Like Me*. The repetition of the first and third line of the first stanza is a continual reminder to the reader of the message of the poem: that only through real empathy can we reach understanding.

Acknowledgments

There have been many people that have influenced me in writing this book. In fact, probably too many to name. But I surely would like to try.

In the fall of my freshman year at St. Peter's College (now University) in Jersey City, NJ, President John Fitzgerald Kennedy was assassinated on November 22, 1963. He encouraged my generation to heed the call to action. ("If not us, who? If not now, when?").

On September 22, 1965, I was fortunate enough to be one of 500 students and professors who were in the auditorium in Dineen Hall at St. Peter's College to see and hear Dr. Martin Luther King Jr. address the Michaelmas Convocation with a speech titled, "The American Dream." He was assassinated on April 4, 1968, right before my graduation from Saint Peter's, where I had heard him speak less than three years before.

The words of the speeches and the autobiography of Frederick Douglas, and one quote, in particular, "If there is no struggle, there is no progress."

From the report of the continued suffering of the Black man in a white world told in books like John Howard Griffin's *Black Like Me* to the real suffering related by Eldridge Cleaver in *Soul on Ice* "The racist conscience of America is such that murder does not register as murder, really, unless the victim is white."

Richard Wright's *Native Son*, and Ralph Ellison's *Invisible Man*, works of amazing power and poignancy, brought the true meaning of discrimination into sharper focus for me.

The books and writings of Ta-Nehisi Coates (*Between the World and Me, We Were Eight Years in Power*) provided facts and context, and challenged my own preconceptions about race and assisted me to better understand the struggle of African Americans for full equality.

Emanuel Acho's *Uncomfortable Conversations with a Black Man*, directly challenged me to write this book of poetry by showing me the wisdom of Dr. Martin Luther King's words "In the end, we will remember not the words of our enemies but the silence of our friends."

[. . .]

Dr. Ibrim X. Kendi's *How to Be an Antiracist* and *Stamped from the Beginning*, both books added further clarity to a fuller understanding of life in a country where "normal" is a relative word for far too many.

The poetry of Langston Hughes, Jericho Brown (*The Tradition*), Kevin Young (*Book of Hours, The Grey Album: On the Blackness of Blackness*), Hanif Willis Abdurraqib (*The Crown Ain't Worth Much*), and Kendrick Lamar (*Damn*) inspired me more than I can explain. The simple eloquence of Langston Hughes, the powerful narratives of Kendrick Lamar, and the inventive use of form and simple words to tell profound truths of Jericho Brown; and finally the honor of being in the house for the readings of Hanif Abdurraqib, Kevin Young and the US Poet Laureate, Natasha Trethewey (*Native Guard*), at Monmouth University on the very topics I have tried to represent with reality and truth in this book—all provided me with inspiration as well as a greater understanding of Dr. Martin Luther King Jr's admonition of "the fierce urgency of now."

And finally, to those who gave me hour after hour of their personal time to talk to me about their observations, experiences, and feelings about racism. Those ideas and ideals gave me inspiration to think deeply and to write honestly. I owe them a deep and profound gratitude.

Thomas Curto Yaccarino who asked me "Can you put dialogue into poetry? If so, then why not have a conversation?"

My fellow poets/craft readers/friends, Susan Martin, Jerry Leary, Nicholas Rocco, Damian Luboch and James C. Ellerbe, who spent time reading and reviewing my manuscript, suggesting revisions, and encouraging me to tell the story in the best way I could.

To my "crew" of five, my former students, for the hours of deep, meaningful and honest Saturday conversations we had over the pandemic months of 2020 and the guidance that they gave me to aim me in the right direction and to help me to say what really had to be said: Anthony Miller, Dr. Elford Rawls-Dill, Aulander Daniels, Marcus McKenzie and Justin Foy; and to Dr. Christopher Harris, Anthony Miller, James C. Ellerbe and Marcus McKenzie who served as "sensitivity readers" to ensure that I didn't step on landmines.

But particularly to Marcus McKenzie, my "adopted" nephew, whose honest discussions with me on what was, for him, a sensitive topic, his unceasing drive, and his dedication to this project, encouraged me to the finish line.

From the bottom of my heart, I thank you all.

Early Praise for *This Conversation*

This poetic volume is not just words, but tools of wisdom. This book is a perfect first step to healing old wounds—one reader and one verbal exchange at a time.

—James C. Ellerbe, poet/founder of Not Enough Words, LLC, and author of *Beyond the Event Horizon*

This book by Christopher Bogart asks crucial questions in our modern-day quest for racial equity and justice. He does so in a series of "conversations" between two ordinary people, white, which go deep into the roots of the whys and wherefores of our present crisis. Each conversation is followed by a poem, which beautifully examines the topic of conversation. These well-crafted poems, of many different styles, could stand on their own, apart from the book, but fit well in its confines. One of the poems, "One Drop", struck me as particularly stark and poignant

> *What sense of science*
> *Makes DNA when*
> *Just one drop*
> *Washes all away*
> *Into the wooden galley's hold*
> *To make them stay –*
> *To pay the price*
> *They've always paid.*

A fair question. And one of many in Bogart's *This Conversation*.

—R. Bremner, author of *Hungry Words, Absurd,* and *Pencil Sketches*

Chris Bogart's book is a lightning rod of discomfort and relevance. It is indeed an allegorical conversation that honestly takes place between the reader and the reader's societal subconscious. *This Conversation* is to be read with an open heart in chest and mirror in hand as it will force readers to

[. . .]

re-examine themselves, as Bogart demands, with more compassion, critical thinking, and candor as they pertain to mending and rectifying the evils of generational racism from all who dare to read this crucial work from a true ally.

—Ras Heru Stewart, CEO of Rebel Ink Publishing
and executive producer of Rhythm & Words: Creative Writing

I thoroughly enjoyed reading this book. It covers not only all the topics a conversation like this would have, it also provides different perspectives on each topic with glimpses of some of the culture that a lot of Americans have no idea exists. The placement of the individual poems within the dialogue, I feel, gives additional yet powerful meaning beyond the dialogue itself. The imagery of one of the main characters scratching off the wet beer sticker with his fingernail, and the movements of the two characters as they converse while holding their beers, are spot on.

Anytime the topic of racism, or BLM, comes up in the future, I will now feel empowered to try to have this conversation myself. And I'll be sure to recommend this book, as well.

—Michael Borrero, software engineer

This Conversation…not only enriched the academic environment of Monmouth University, but also served to challenge our collective intellectual development. For me, Chris Bogart was one of the great highlights of the day, showing us the excellence of our graduate students. His excellent caliber of creative work is a vehicle for having discussions around race. It is a rare contribution that is beautifully written and of such practical importance.

—Geoffrey Fouad, PhD, assistant Professor of Geography
and organizer of Interdisciplinary Conference on Race,
Monmouth University

About the Author

 Christopher Bogart is a working poet and writer who has earned an MA in Creative Writing, and is presently working on an MFA, at Monmouth University.

In 2015, Bogart was chosen as First Runner Up for Monmouth University's inaugural Joyce Carol Oates Award for Excellence in Fiction, Poetry, and Creative Non-Fiction. In 2017, he was chosen as one of two finalists for The Brian Turner Literary Prize for Fiction. In 2018, his chapbook about the Yuma 14, titled *14: Antología del Sonoran*, was awarded third place in The Poetry Box Chapbook Prize and was published in October of 2018 by The Poetry Box. He was then nominated for a Pushcart Prize for his poem, "Abraham Morales Hernandez."

In April of 2020, The Poetry Box published his chapbook, *Breakpoint* about America in the era of Donald Trump, and a full-length book of poetry in May about the plight of Central American migrants, *The Eater of Dreams*.

On August 1, 2005, he had presented a paper on the importance of poetry in the teaching of literature and writing to the Oxford Round Table at the Oxford Union Debate Hall at Oxford University.

He is presently working on his first novel, tentatively titled *The Beast*, about the plight of two Central American teenagers who flee poverty and crime in search of a better life in the United States.

About The Poetry Box®

The Poetry Box, a boutique publishing company in Portland, Oregon, provides a platform for both established and emerging poets to share their words with the world through beautiful printed books and chapbooks.

Feel free to visit the online bookstore (thePoetryBox.com), where you'll find more titles including:

14: Antología del Sonoran by Christopher Bogart

Breakpoint by Christopher Bogart

The Eater of Dreams by Christopher Bogart

A Democracy Divided by Ralph J. Long Jr.

Songs of an Indomitable Spirit by Michael B. Carroll Jr.

The Dichotomy between Light & Dark by Michael B. Carroll Jr.

Picking Scabs from the Body History by Joanne Godley

Gospel Gone Blues by Jimmie Ware

Let's Hear It For the Horses by Tricia Knoll

What We Bring Home by Susan Coultrap-McQuin

Beneath the Gravel Weight of Stars by Mimi German

Earth Resonance: Poems for a Viable Future by Sam Love

Contraband by Juan Pablo Mobili

and more . . .

www.ingramcontent.com/pod-product-compliance
Lightning Source LLC
LaVergne TN
LVHW020435080526
838202LV00055B/5189